Jackie Robinson

JOSH GREGORY

Children's Press®
An Imprint of Scholastic Inc.

Content Consultant
Barry Wilner
Associated Press
New York City, New York

Library of Congress Cataloging-in-Publication Data
Gregory, Josh.
  Jackie Robinson / Josh Gregory.
    pages cm. — (A True Book)
  Includes bibliographical references and index.
  ISBN 978-0-531-21598-2 (library binding) — ISBN 978-0-531-21760-3 (paperback)
  1. Robinson, Jackie, 1919–1972. 2. African American baseball players—United States—
Biography—Juvenile literature. I. Title.
  GV865.R6G75 2015
  796.357092—dc23 [B]   2014044749

© 2016 Scholastic Inc.
All rights reserved. Published in 2016 by Children's Press, an imprint of Scholastic Inc. Published
simultaneously in Canada. Printed in China 62
SCHOLASTIC, CHILDREN'S PRESS, A TRUE BOOK™, and associated logos are trademarks and/or
registered trademarks of Scholastic Inc.
1 2 3 4 5 6 7 8 9 10 R 25 24 23 22 21 20 19 18 17 16

**Front cover: Jackie Robinson in his
Brooklyn Dodgers uniform**

**Back cover: Robinson holding his
Baseball Hall of Fame plaque**

Find the Truth!

Everything you are about to read is true *except* for one of the sentences on this page.

Which one is **TRUE**?

T or F Jackie Robinson left college to play baseball for the Brooklyn Dodgers.

T or F Robinson played football before becoming a professional baseball player.

Find the answers in this book.

Contents

Willie Mays

THE BIG TRUTH!

Jackie Robinson
(right) meets with civil
rights leader Martin
Luther King Jr.

4 An American Hero

What effect did Robinson have on
civil rights in the United States? **35**

In 1984, Robinson
was awarded the
Presidential Medal of
Freedom, the highest
honor for a U.S. civilian.

Jackie Robinson forever changed the way African Americans were treated in professional sports.

CHAPTER 1

A Young Athlete

The United States was divided in the mid-20th century. Slavery had ended in 1865. African Americans were legally free, but they were not treated equally. Black and white Americans were **segregated**. Even professional sports were kept separate. No matter how good a black baseball player was, he could not play in the major leagues. This would all begin to change when a man named Jackie Robinson took the field in 1947.

 Jackie Robinson was chosen as an All-Star in six of his ten major league seasons.

Born in Georgia

Jackie was born Jack Roosevelt Robinson on January 31, 1919, in Cairo, Georgia. He was the youngest member of his family, with three older brothers and one older sister. Like most black families living in the South at the time, the Robinsons faced difficulties. Jackie's grandfather had been a slave. His father, Jerry, earned just $12 a month working on a farm.

Jackie's siblings were named Edgar, Frank, Mack, and Willa Mae.

Though Jackie's family did not always have it easy, he had a good childhood surrounded by loving relatives.

Jackie (second from left) poses with his siblings and his mother at around age 6.

Moving to California

When Jackie was about six months old, Jerry left the family to look for a better job. He never came back. Jackie's mother, Mallie, moved the family to Pasadena, California. Most of the other people in Pasadena were white. The Robinsons faced racism and segregation. Mallie worked long hours as a maid to support the family. While she was working, Jackie's siblings looked after him.

At the 1936 Olympics, Mack Robinson (left, front) finished second in the 200-meter race after another American, Jesse Owens (far right).

Jackie's brother Mack won a silver medal in track at the 1936 Olympic Games in Germany.

A Family of Athletes

Growing up, Jackie and his siblings all enjoyed playing sports. The Robinsons were natural athletes. Jackie was always the player that other kids wanted on their team. By the time he started high school, he was a well-rounded athlete. He became a star on the football, baseball, and basketball teams at John Muir Technical High School. He also ran track.

Off to College

A white student with Jackie's athletic abilities might have easily won a **scholarship** at a major university. However, most big colleges did not accept many black students at the time. Jackie decided to attend nearby Pasadena Junior College instead. There, he continued to star in sports. He even led the school to championships in football, baseball, and basketball.

Jackie attended Pasadena Junior College for two years.

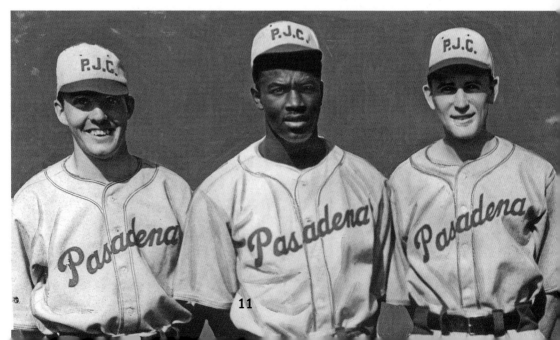

Bigger colleges could no longer ignore Jackie's skills. The University of California, Los Angeles (UCLA) offered him a scholarship in 1939. There, he continued to show athletic excellence. He became the first player in UCLA history to earn a **letter** in four sports in the same year. He was also the top scorer on the basketball team and was considered one of the best college football players in the country.

Jackie (No. 28) shakes off defenders as he runs the ball during a UCLA football game.

Jackie competes in a long jump event at a UCLA track meet.

Big Changes

Between playing four sports and keeping up with his studies, Jackie was very busy at UCLA. However, he still found time for a social life. He met a nursing student at the university named Rachel Isum. They soon began dating.

Unfortunately, Jackie's college career was cut short. In spring 1941, he left school to find a job. Mallie was struggling to make ends meet, and Jackie wanted to help the family.

The United States was drawn into World War II after the Japanese military launched a surprise attack on the Pearl Harbor U.S. Naval Base on December 7, 1941.

CHAPTER 2

From Basic Training to Spring Training

Robinson soon joined a football team in Hawaii. It was one of the few sports teams that allowed black players to participate alongside white players. In December 1941, he returned to California, where he could be closer to his family. However, that same month, the United States began fighting in World War II. The U.S. Army needed strong, young men to fight. Robinson was **drafted** in early 1942.

Robinson (left) tries on heavyweight boxing champion Joe Louis's boxing glove as Louis holds Robinson's bat at an event in 1946.

Lieutenant Robinson

In the army, Robinson once again faced racism and segregation. After he finished basic training, he wanted to become an officer. Though he was qualified, the army would not let him into Officer Candidate School (OCS) because he was black. Boxing champion Joe Louis was also in the army at the time. He heard about Robinson's problem. Louis used his influence to convince the army to admit Robinson into OCS.

Robinson finished OCS as a lieutenant. Because of segregation in the military, all the men under his command were black. They often faced racist treatment. In 1944, a bus driver ordered Robinson to move back on a bus, farther from white passengers. Robinson refused. As a result, he was accused of breaking military law. He was tried and found not guilty, but the trial affected Robinson deeply. He asked to be released from service and was **honorably discharged** later that year.

As an officer, Robinson often stood up for the rights of his men.

17

Joining the Monarchs

Left without a job or a position in the military, Robinson needed a way to earn money. He knew about the baseball teams playing in the Negro Leagues. Negro League teams were owned and operated by black people. They were also made up entirely of black players. This was the only way for African Americans to participate in professional baseball during segregation.

Black baseball stars around the nation began playing for Negro League teams in the early 20th century.

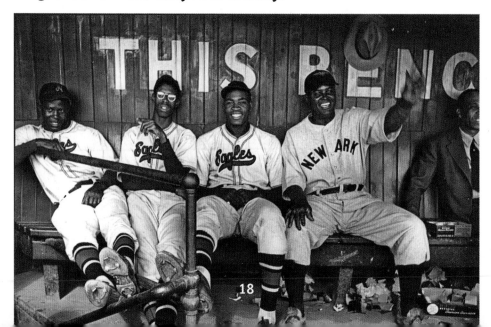

Robinson (front row, third from left) poses for a team photo with the rest of the Monarchs.

Robinson thought that the Negro Leagues could be a good way to make money. After leaving the army, Robinson called the Kansas City Monarchs team in the Negro League to arrange a tryout. He impressed the team right away and began playing for them in spring 1945. Almost immediately, he emerged as one of the Monarchs' biggest stars.

The team bus became like a second home for many Negro League players.

Life in the Negro Leagues

Playing baseball in the Negro Leagues did not lead to a glamorous lifestyle. Players did not make nearly as much money as white players in the major leagues. In addition, they faced a hard travel schedule, going from city to city, playing game after game. They were often refused service at hotels and restaurants along the way. This left the players to get what little rest they could on the bus between games.

Fed Up

After a few months of playing for the Monarchs, Robinson was tired of the difficult lifestyle. He wasn't making enough money to support his family the way he wanted to. He started thinking about leaving pro baseball behind. He planned to move back to California, marry Rachel, and find a new career. Little did he know that circumstances were about to change.

The Monarchs were founded in 1920 and played until 1965.

Robinson was a standout player during his time with the Monarchs.

No African American had played for the major leagues since the end of the 19th century.

The Road to the Majors

In the 1940s, big changes were taking place behind the scenes of major league baseball. Under pressure from **activists**, the league had agreed early in the decade to allow teams to hire black players. League leaders had believed that no team would actually go through with signing a black player. However, they were about to be proven wrong.

There were only 16 major league baseball teams when Jackie Robinson made his debut in 1947.

A Plan to Integrate

Branch Rickey, president of the Brooklyn Dodgers, wanted to **integrate** the league. He began sending scouts to watch Negro League players in action. Rickey knew, however, that the first black major league player would need more than just baseball skills. The player would also need to be strong enough to stand up to the racism he was sure to face.

The Dodgers had a history of star players, including, from left to right, Arky Vaughan, Dolph Camilli, Billy Herman, and Pee Wee Reese.

24

Branch Rickey

Branch Rickey began his sports career playing football and baseball while still in college. After graduating, he began a long career as a coach, manager, and executive in pro baseball. Rickey was disgusted by the way black athletes were harassed by fans, opponents, and even teammates. He hoped that integration in the major leagues could change the way African American athletes were treated.

Rickey (left) meets with Dodgers manager Leo Durocher (right) and scout Clyde Sukeforth (center), who helped recruit Jackie Robinson from the Negro Leagues.

Scouting for a Star

Rickey's scouts pretended to look for players for a new, all-black Dodgers team. They watched Negro League games and learned what they could about the players' lives. Then they reported back to Rickey. After considering some of the nation's top black ballplayers, Rickey determined that Robinson was the right man for the job. He was not only a great player. His actions while he was in the army showed he wouldn't back down when confronting racism.

A Fateful Meeting

In August 1945, one of Rickey's scouts approached Robinson to set up a meeting with the Dodgers president. He told Robinson that Rickey was creating a new all-black team. Robinson was intrigued. Such an opportunity might be exactly what he needed. At the meeting, Robinson was stunned when Rickey told him the truth: He wanted him to become the first black player in the major leagues.

Rickey and Robinson formed a friendship that lasted for many years.

Robinson knew the challenges he would face as the only black player in the league. He would have to contend with racist players, fans, and coaches. Rickey explained that they had chosen him because they thought he could handle the pressure. Robinson agreed that he was up to the challenge. He realized that he had an incredible opportunity. His actions could change not just baseball but race relations throughout the nation.

Robinson signs a contract to play for the Royals in 1945.

Jackie and Rachel Robinson were married on February 10, 1946, in Los Angeles.

A Smooth Transition

Rickey planned to ease Robinson into the league to avoid facing too much resistance. Robinson would start out playing for the Montreal Royals, a **farm team** for the Dodgers.

Robinson's personal life was changing, too. In February 1946, he and Rachel were married. Soon after, he was on his way to spring training with the Royals.

Though he was unfair to Robinson at first, Royals manager Clay Hopper (left) eventually came to respect Robinson's abilities on the field.

Rising to the Challenge

Robinson ran into trouble right off the bat. The Royals' manager did not want him on the team. Rickey told the manager that he had no choice. Robinson played well and soon gained the respect of both the manager and his teammates. Baseball fans and opposing teams continued to insult him whenever he took the field. However, this didn't stop Robinson. He led the Royals to a championship that season.

Meeting the Dodgers

In 1947, the Royals and Dodgers went to spring training together. This gave Robinson a chance to play with the Dodgers. Some of the Dodgers complained. In response, Rickey threatened to fire them. When spring training was over, Rickey announced that Robinson would join the Dodgers for the coming season.

Robinson stretches to catch a fly ball in Montreal.

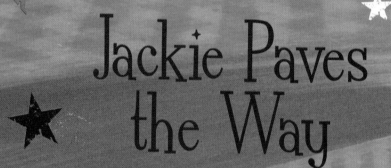

THE BIG TRUTH!

Jackie Paves the Way

After Jackie Robinson made his major league debug, other teams began hiring black players. Many of these players were Negro League stars, and they went on to become major league legends.

Larry Doby
Larry Doby began playing for the Cleveland Indians later in the same season that Robinson joined the Dodgers. This made Doby the second player to break baseball's color barrier. A veteran star of the Negro Leagues, Doby was known for his powerful hitting.

Satchel Paige

Satchel Paige joined the Cleveland Indians in 1948, when he was well over 40 years old. Paige is considered one of the greatest pitchers in baseball history. He was famous for his stunts. For example, sometimes he would intentionally let three players get hits to load the bases, then strike out the fourth player.

Willie Mays

Willie Mays started playing in the Negro Leagues when he was just 16 years old. He joined the New York Giants in 1951, at age 20, and was named **rookie** of the year. During his 22-year career in the majors, he hit 660 home runs.

Hank Aaron

Home run king Hank Aaron played in the Negro Leagues for a few months in 1952 before moving on to the majors. He hit 755 home runs during his major league career, a record that stood until 2007.

Robinson (right) poses with teammates, from left to right, John Jorgensen, Pee Wee Reese, and Ed Stanky during his very first major league game in 1947.

An American Hero

On April 15, 1947, Robinson took the field as a Dodger for the first time. Robinson heard both cheers and insults as he stepped up to the plate. Some of his teammates showed him support, though others did not entirely accept him. Unfortunately, it wasn't the best game of Robinson's career. Under the pressure of such a historic moment, he started off with a slump that went on for several games. It wouldn't last, though.

Robinson joined the Dodgers as a first baseman. He later switched to second base.

Rookie of the Year

Robinson didn't give up. Soon he was back to his old ways. It wasn't long before he became known as one of the best players in the league. Fans of all races packed stadiums across the country to watch him play. He was especially known for his powerful hitting and daring stolen base attempts. For these efforts, Robinson was named the league's first rookie of the year.

An umpire signals that Robinson is safe as he slides into third base during a game against the New York Yankees.

On the road, Robinson often had to stay in separate hotels or eat in separate restaurants from his white teammates.

Fans watch as Robinson gets a hit during a 1955 game.

Dealing With Racists

Robinson's talent didn't stop people from treating him poorly. Members of opposing teams insulted him and attempted to harm him. Some teams threatened not to play the Dodgers at all. Angry fans threw things at him. He even received death threats. However, Robinson never fought back. He believed people would use a fight as an excuse to say that black players shouldn't be in the league. Robinson held his head high and continued playing.

A Legendary Career

Over the following seasons, the Dodgers were one of the best teams in baseball. This was thanks in large part to Robinson's remarkable abilities. In 1949, he was named the league's most valuable player. In 1947, 1949, 1952, and 1953, he led the Dodgers all the way to the World Series. The New York Yankees defeated them each time. Finally, in 1955, the Dodgers defeated the Yankees to win the championship.

Timeline of Robinson's Life

January 31, 1919

Jackie Robinson is born in Cairo, Georgia.

1945

Robinson begins playing baseball in the Negro Leagues.

Role Model

During his time playing for the Dodgers, Robinson became a national hero. He was an inspiration to young African American athletes across the country. He also offered guidance to the many black players who joined the league after him. He discussed how to deal with **prejudice** and other troubles in the league. He also often spoke out in public about racism and political issues.

1962
Robinson is named to the Baseball Hall of Fame in his first year of eligibility.

April 15, 1947
Robinson breaks the color barrier by playing his first game for the Brooklyn Dodgers.

Robinson reads the comics page of the newspaper with his family in 1957.

Leaving the Game Behind

In 1957, at the age of 38, Robinson retired from baseball. After a long career as a pro athlete, he was growing too old to play the way he used to. He also wanted to spend more time with his family. During his time with the Dodgers, he and Rachel had had three children—Sharon, David, and Jackie Jr.

Civil Rights Leader

Even though he was retired, Robinson stayed in the public eye. He knew that he could use his fame to accomplish important things for African Americans. By the late 1950s, the **civil rights** movement was in full swing. Robinson became an important spokesman for the movement. He helped raise funds for the National Association for the Advancement of Colored People (NAACP). He also met with civil rights leaders such as Malcolm X and Martin Luther King Jr.

Robinson (right) meets with Dr. Martin Luther King Jr. in 1962.

Mourning a Hero

Not long after retiring, Robinson was diagnosed with diabetes. This illness caused him a number of health issues. Among other things, Robinson's heart weakened. He died of a heart attack in October 1972 at the age of 53. Across the nation, people mourned the baseball pioneer and American hero.

In 1997, the Major League Baseball organization retired Robinson's number, 42, across the entire league. No other player could claim the number as his own.

Robinson was inducted into the Baseball Hall of Fame in 1962.

The Los Angeles Dodgers listen to the national anthem at a 2007 game celebrating the 60th anniversary of Jackie Robinson's major league debut.

Gone but Not Forgotten

In 2004, Major League Baseball declared April 15 would be celebrated each year as Jackie Robinson Day. On this day, all players in the league wear number 42 on their jerseys to honor him. For his abilities on the field and his bravery against racism, Robinson is remembered as one of the most important players in baseball history. He continues to be an inspiration to anyone who has ever struggled against prejudice. ★

Number of seasons Robinson played for the Kansas City Monarchs: 1

Number of seasons Robinson played for the Montreal Royals: 1

Number of seasons Robinson played for the Brooklyn Dodgers: 10

Total home runs Robinson hit during his major league career: 137

Total bases stolen by Robinson during his major league career: 197

Number of times Robinson led the Dodgers to the World Series: 5

Number of times Robinson led the Dodgers to victory in the World Series: 1

Robinson's career batting average: .311

Did you find the truth?

F Jackie Robinson left college to play baseball for the Brooklyn Dodgers.

T Robinson played football before becoming a professional baseball player.

Resources

Books

Robinson, Sharon. *Jackie Robinson: American Hero*. New York: Scholastic, 2013.

Robinson, Sharon. *Promises to Keep: How Jackie Robinson Changed America*. New York: Scholastic, 2004.

Teitelbaum, Michael. *Jackie Robinson: Champion for Equality*. New York: Sterling, 2010.

Visit this Scholastic Web site for more information on Jackie Robinson:
★ www.factsfornow.scholastic.com
Enter the keywords **Jackie Robinson**

Important Words

activists (AK-ti-vists) — people who work for change

civil rights (SIV-uhl RITES) — the individual rights that all members of a democratic society have to freedom and equal treatment under the law

drafted (DRAF-tid) — made to join the armed forces

farm team (FARM TEEM) — a minor league baseball team that provides training and experience to players, who can go on to join an associated major league team

honorably discharged (AH-nur-uh-blee DIS-charjd) — released from the military with a rating of good or excellent for his or her service

integrate (IN-tuh-grate) — to include people of all races

letter (LET-ur) — an award earned for reaching a certain standard in sports or other school activities

prejudice (PREJ-uh-dis) — an immovable, unreasonable, or unfair opinion about someone based on the person's race, religion, or other characteristic

rookie (RUK-ee) — an athlete who is in his or her first season with a professional sports team

scholarship (SKAH-lur-ship) — money given to pay for a person to go to college or to follow a course of study

segregated (SEG-ruh-gay-tid) — separated or kept apart

Index

Page numbers in **bold** indicate illustrations.

About the Author

Josh Gregory has written more than 80 books covering a wide range of subjects. He lives in Chicago, Illinois.

10/13

Atlanta-Fulton Public Library